Time's Tyranny

poems by

Jean P. Moore

Finishing Line Press
Georgetown, Kentucky

Time's Tyranny

ACKNOWLEDGMENTS

All rights to previously published poems have reverted to me. The poems are:

"Up on Church Road," "Amber Eyes," "In the garden of the bibliotecca where I
last saw you," *SN Review*, 2014.
"*Views of the Valley*, page 76," "The River" (previously published as "Evening,"),
"Dancing with My Mother" (finalist), *Women's Voices of the 21st Century*, a
publication of the Greenwich CT branch of the National League of American Pen
Women, 2013.
"Hiking the Cobble," *upstreet*, 2005.
"Block Island," *Adanna*, 2014.
"On the Train from Verona," *The Timberline Review*, 2016.

Publisher: Leah Maines

Editor: Christen Kincaid

Cover Art: "Church Road in Winter," Steven J. Rubin

Author Photo: Chuan Ding

Cover Design: Elizabeth Maines McCleavy

Printed in the USA on acid-free paper.
Order online: www.finishinglinepress.com
            also available on amazon.com

Author inquiries and mail orders:
Finishing Line Press
P. O. Box 1626
Georgetown, Kentucky 40324
U. S. A.

Table of Contents

Views of the Valley, page 76 1

Up on Church Road 2

The River 3

Ancestral Fault Line 4

Hiking the Cobble 5

Going Farther Still 6

Healing 7

Early Spring, Late Spring 1, Late Spring 2 8

Girls in the Garden (Rondeau for Granddaughters) 9

Two: 1 Their Grandmother, 2 Their Frenzy 10

The order of things 11

Dancing with My Mother 12

Amber Eyes 13

Trapper 14

Block Island 15

On a Day 16

Now when we are old 17

September 18

Helios 19

In the garden of the biblioteca where I last saw you 20

I Don't Know You 21

In Response to Carpet Bombing: Among the Crèches 22

Leaving Aleppo 23

The yellow leaves of fall 24

On the train to the city 26

On the train from Verona 27

Atop a hill 28

For Steve

There, my barn and house
sugar maple young and spindly
familiar hills, the schoolhouse too
I know, but

Who is that woman standing
proud in my yard, by a black horse,
both standing in the snow?

You in your long dark dress not even
a coat for cover, are you cold?
I think I see a smile, but
faintly, you are fading
even as the camera holds you—
in the mind's eye a life floats
up—breath, birth, girlhood,
marriage, children, old age
a good death if you were lucky, but
your heart—the mystery
your deepest hopes and dreams
what you wished for, what you loved and lost—
and what you told the world—
the mystery

Who is that woman in my yard
image seared upon a page?

Will another see me ages hence
standing in the snow and wonder?

Up on Church Road

Up on the hill by the church
lie the bones of soldiers.
Old or new they are eternity's bones,
borne of tyranny and greed—
of those who in life they believed.

Old bones or new mingling with tears
some long dry and turned to dust
others freshly placed.

Today is the Fourth of July.
We on Jerusalem Road
wait for fireworks.

Instead, encircling us
is the sparkle of fireflies
a barrage of light, like stars,
heaven come to earth
nothing else in sight
just the shimmer of these wild things

who know the tyranny of time
whose only greed is for life.

The River

At my sink, I look out the kitchen window to the river,
pale in the lowering light.

Soon Ophelia goes floating by, famous tresses framing her sleeping face,
right behind is Shelley's Harriet, fists in a knot, frustrated and angry, to the
end.

Now Virginia—not floating so much as bobbing (those stones, you know),
next comes Sylvia, why this watery way, I'm not sure, but there she is,
her oven pulling her along.

And following closely, Anne, just after last lunch, her struggle done.
It's quite a crowd, really.
Craning my neck, I see them all, piling up on the rocks under the bridge.

The thought occurs, what if I could reverse the water's flow,
send them back, to endure a while longer?
Would not time have eased their sorrow?
Could they not have reached a later age and been happy then—
grandchildren, great nieces, nephews, sitting on their laps?

And could they not have shown the way,
marked the hazardous shoals,
for those younger, yet to come,
still in the throes of it?

Ancestral Fault Line

Everything's a sacrament this time of day,
shards of pale light making even a modest kitchen
a cathedral.

Standing at the sink, she rinses her cup,
letting the water spill onto her hands.
Reaching for the white cloth on the counter, she wipes them dry.

How many years ago now since those sacramental waters
washed away her sins?

How many infants since has she seen squirm against
the cold rush so unlike the familiar and
warm amniotic waters?

Oh those disobedient babes, luckily
thrown the rescue rope of redemption
against the havoc of the womb.

Hiking the Cobble

Today the hope comes again unbidden—
On these high rocks what could be more divine
Than to see an eagle soar near heaven.
Then would she know, then would she have her sign.
As she hikes, the sky is crisp and cloud-clear.
Though in all that she sees no eagles fly,
Still, on the breeze a common crow glides near.
His wings glisten blue-black, then a loud cry,
She stands watch, feels an echo in the bone.
Her heart opens a path to a root knowing.
This common crow in his own way has shown
What she grasped once but lost in the going.
To equally embrace eagle and crow,
This is the true sign, this much she must know.

Going Farther Still

Sitting on the edge of my Adirondack, leaning all the way back, head touching board, I have no choice but to look up.

There above the trees, a dragonfly. You wouldn't think it soars so high, but it does. So many summers behind me now—and once again, there, wings glistening.

When I was a child I saw it all. I'd put a hand in the bushes and pull out a bird, put a hand in the ground and pull out a rabbit, no really, I did.

When I was a child time was the space between going out in the morning and coming back at dusk to my mother's whistle.

Now it is the space between going out and going farther still. No more rabbits in their nests, but there's magic yet.

Healing

All around the rush of summer, brooks tumbling, gardens yielding, bees tousling the young heads of June.

Soon so soon the picnics of July, concerts to attend, games to play, friends to see, then the rush of August as all living things heed
a new cast of light…more and more must be done.

Not for me this summer.

I have lain first then sat, sat and watched nature hum, friends scurry, attend, intend while I sitting strive for
Patience

from bed to chair to standing on my own I walk into the solace of September

Coming down Jerusalem Road I listen to the sugar maples making ready their finale, I look beyond to see a silver mist separating hill and field

In October the maple outside my window glows red in waning sunlight I wait
then open the kitchen door at six, leaning against the screen I hear the bells sing out
Amazing
Grace

Early Spring

A bureaucratic robin sits atop
the blossomed cherry tree and
keeps watch on the hill where
everywhere his kind strut—on the ground,
in the trees.

You can enter, they say, but you cannot stay.

Late Spring 1

On this late spring morning
dim blossoms lie fixed on the wet pavement—
a scrapbook's pressed flowers.
Her heart peers out from behind still winter's curtain.
Then the goslings, baby yellow, downy brown,
and she's undone.

Throw open the curtains, open the windows.
Still enough blossoms on the tree in this spring yet.
Spring yet.
She will stay here.
No next season for her.

Late Spring 2

Now we track in the deep mud of mangled spring
No more apple white or cherry red
Now the flower mud as dark as winter's thaw, only a moment ago.
This mud promise is of yet more fleeting sun.

Girls in the Garden
(Rondeau for Granddaughters)

In the garden sweat and toil
So slow at first hands in soil
Then it happens, life is a race
A profusion how to keep pace
All accomplished just for the girls

Tomatoes parsley and basil
All will be well ever the whirl
If by late June girls in their place
In the garden

Year by year there they dance and twirl
"Life's fleeting," I am left to mull
But here I dig, all for this grace
Enna, Maddie, and Lilly in lace
Playing, running, singing, my girls
In the garden.

Two: 1 Their Grandmother, 2 Their Frenzy

1 Their Grandmother

Sees them in the backyard run
up and down, many times,
never stopping to catch
their breath, never tiring, they go
on and on.

Held in the stark light of August, there they will remain
in my mind's eye, I cannot escape it—
I must move on to November and further still—
It is true. Their joy
exhausts me

2 Their Frenzy

Into the garden they go, plucking at the roses—no,
leave the new ones—I cry
to no avail.

Now fallen apples go reeling
into the brook the girls are in
a frenzy

running up and down rolling down the hill
never mind the itch of grass
only a cool bath can cure
only now this moment
rolling down this hill.

It is all that matters.

The order of things

When you were eight you went
to summer camp. I cleaned the house
and fluffed the pillows. I sat neatly and admired
the order of things.

When you came home I threw you
in the shower clothes and all to
wash away the traces of your absence.

Then I admired you throwing
 toys, tossing pillows, clutter everywhere.

This summer I went through every
drawer and closet, casting off all
I did not need.

Then I cleaned the walls and floors,
I washed the rugs and sheets—I would not leave
an old woman's cluttered house.

I admired the order of things, but this time
you would not disturb it.

Dancing with My Mother

That night it was just the two of us
I curled my spine as best I could to sleep in the chair beside your bed
Soon you who had not walked in weeks rose to tap me on the shoulder
You put out your two slender hands and clasped my own in yours
Then with only the music we two made we danced over chair and bed over
whatever was in our way we danced to the rhythm of your breathing light
and loving as your touch had always been.

We danced and outside your window the moon shone on mounds of snow
lighting a path to where you would go

without me.

Amber Eyes

Who could resist those amber eyes?
In spite of the chromosomal divide,
he speaks to me, soothsaying
his message of accommodation. Let me sleep before
your fire, eat your scraps, and I will be there
when you are left, comfort you in grief, warm you
in the cold and keep harm from your door.

This was the pact made long ago before he
began to prowl among the appliances.

Trapper

He was a stray before we got him,
more skinny than sleek, and his shiny
black fur had bare places
where the wounds had been.

That first day he rubbed his back
deep into the carpet. Home, I almost
heard him say, home. Happy to be
safe, warm, and fed.

He wasn't used to a leash and collar, and
walking up Jerusalem Road was a contest
I was sure to win, not with "heel"
but with a good firm tug.

Once on Cobble Hill, he slipped his collar and
bolted for the high fields, his muscles
gleaming in the sun. I laughed from some place
deep within and watched him go.

I lured him back with treats, placing the collar
and leash around his neck, like the trapper
I'd become. Years have passed since then,
but the Cobble's still there.

I know he wants to try again, and I want him to.
Who wouldn't?

To be that strong, run that fast,
and be that free?

Block Island

You kept the postcard from that trip
 tucked way back in a drawer—

it had a picture of the bright chairs,
atop the hill looking out to sea.

We took the ferry and were seasick
the whole way. It was after the season,

and everyone was gone. At first we
thought there was nothing to do,

but we made love all night long. We didn't
stop until we were crazy for it to end.

I wrote, one day, years from now,
we'll return,

sit in these same chairs, too old
probably to do much else.

Now I pull out that card and wonder
when we are going back.

On a Day

One day on a day we cannot know
You or I will no longer be here to
Remember the night you spilled
Wine on the tablecloth
We use only for special occasions.

If it is I, I will sink my face into it,
And lament the anger I let slip as you
Raised the first glass of the night.

You who so lovingly prepared for this
Night so different from all others
You who left a card on the table for me
To find when I sat down.

I will wish to have that moment back and
To tell you, it is nothing, nothing, and I will wipe
The spot with a wet cloth and soothe your
Feelings with a light touch on your shoulder.

Now when we are old

I was with you when your
mother died and I asked if you
were going to be a good shiva boy and
you were not and I held you to me
through your grief.

When I was broken and could
not walk you stayed by me but not
with me until one night when you
gently pressed me to you and
brought me back to life.

Now when we are old I remember the time
on Block Island when there was nothing
to do so we made love all night to amuse
ourselves. I never knew such passion

until now when we are old and I have never
needed or wanted you more.

September

September is my bardo
between what was and what will be

without you.

I watch the sugar maple release
a pale yellow leaf, I follow its
path to the ground.

I will drink tea, play music, read.
a lovely afternoon some would say.

Later I will lie listening to the
for sale sign swinging on its hinges in
the night.

The fire's embers will stir to no avail.

The wind will torment
thinning trees.

The sun will rise and
try to proclaim its might.

The hawk, no fool, will
continue on its way.

Helios

Morning is a memory
of sweet breezes and
weak yet welcome
sun.

But morning's progress
into day
slowly burned the breeze
away

'til there was nothing

but white sun and heat
and the promise that
would not keep.

In the garden of the biblioteca where I last saw you

Zapata with a black telephone and
a computer sat at the stone table
trying to make a connection.

Walt Whitman stood by him
putting his images
into a plastic bag

while nearby Lorca
with notebook and pen searched
for words to make it right.

A sailor looked up to the
mountains, shielding his
eyes from the sun,

and a young girl ran among the
columns playing hide and seek
alone.

...

In the shade, two Americans are drinking
water from plastic bottles,
escaping from the heat.

The bougainvillea goes unnoticed
while the juniper by the door
leans toward the light.

The courtyard fountain
whispers
your name.

I Don't Know You

I don't know you but you are in my blood and bones.
I lift my hand, but it is you who open the door

You who came before crossed an ocean as vast as space
into the unknown. You followed hope into the new.

The New World. What words passed you lips when you saw her?

The silence of prayer, only the wind made a sound as you passed
the light held high by her arm outstretched in the harbor.
How you must have marveled at what you saw.

Nothing would stop you as you entered into life as far from all you
knew as the stars in the foreign black night sky. Not the jostling,
not the words you knew were curses but that you did not understand,

not the power of the loneliness that bent you in half. Nothing would stop
you.
And so you my brother my sister my father my mother of centuries past—
you gave this miracle to me.

You are the body and soul that are my body and soul.

In Response to Carpet Bombing: Among the Crèches

The Tagua Palm Nut:

The brown nut falls from the palm.
In time, animals eat away the husk
to reveal a kernel hardened by seasons
of sun, wind, and rain.
In the husk all along is the kernel to be scooped
into the hands of the one who will fashion it,
who will whittle it, carve it, until it is at last made
into what the world craves, objects of commerce,
trinkets, figurines, jewelry…vegetable ivory it is called.
But sometimes it is transformed into what has lain
dormant in the ivory nut all along.

The Tagua Palm Nut Crèche:

The crèche was one among hundreds,
all lovingly displayed, made of plastic or gold.
There among the multitude cradling the infant
was a singular manger made from the kernel of the nut
that had fallen from the tagua tree,
that had made its journey to here,
among all the others, all proclaiming the arrival
of the prince of peace, he who would one day,
on the back of a donkey, ride into a city
at the crossroads. Humbly, he came in peace.
He comes in peace, the sweet sigh of peace,
for those who are humble and hard and true
enough to seek it.

Leaving Aleppo

They were looking at the camera
the family of four, elderly mother and father,
grown son. The cat crouched on the young man's shoulder
made the foursome, all with eyes dark, looking but seeing no future.

Eyes with hope are not that opaque.

Yet there was the cat. In my mind's eye I saw then the young man
leaning down, scooping the cat up. "Come," he must have said,
lowering his shoulder to let the cat climb up,
beginning their journey of uncertainty.

Is the cat the hope? Was the drive that scooped up
the cat the hope? Surely all is not lost when you leave everything,
when your survival is in doubt, surely there is hope when you leave
with a cat on your shoulder.

Covered in ash, they continue on a battered path. Beneath the grime I
see the clothes of a different life. It is not hard to see him on a field, a
soccer ball rolling between his feet. She has buttoned her once fine coat
as always to the throat. In one hand, the leather bag she once opened
extracting the bill to pay the butcher.

The old man no longer fills his clothes. He walks not expecting to arrive.

I know what it is to be cold and tired in the dark. I have waited on a
tarmac on one foot and then the other to retrieve my bag. I was patient.
A warm bed awaited and home.

But where are they tonight? I allow myself to imagine
three cots and blankets,
a saucer of milk.

The yellow leaves of fall

High atop the yellow leaves in
the upper branches of the
maple by the brook

my small head protrudes, body fragile
as an egg, I swinging,
hold on,
then a snap and
I break
from my narrow perch,
and make
my way down

falling,
falling
rocks below
river waters
running
swiftly by

ah the fall
that made us human
what I nearly missed
a near miss,
the yellow leaves
of fall

all around me now not
the rocks or river
swiftly running by
I am wrapped in the cushion
of the yellow leaves of fall

who would want to miss
what I nearly missed?

We take our chances all—
to be embraced
in the yellow
leaves of fall.

On the train to the city

On the train I turned
to see a girl with her lover
bring a red ribbon from her bag
and pull it round her head.

She tied it in a bow with a little slant,
and I was five again, tangling stray strands of hair
in a rough knot of ribbon, unaccustomed
fingers fumbling so.

My mother helped to sort things out,
and when she lifted me to look, there I was
in the bathroom mirror. Pretty,

I thought, and wanted
all to see the ribbon round
my head and my bright red bow.

Then the train pulled
into the station, the girl was gone,
her lover, too. And I returned
to my forgetting.

On the train from Verona

It was to be a full summer day, opera soon to begin…

In the arena the stage is set for *Aida*—we hear them sing
O terra addio!

We pass Juliet's house and gaze upon her balcony. The city is
a random mix of old and new, history and myth.

We have lunch in an outdoor café of no real distinction and head for the train
to Milan. We have treated ourselves to first class and air conditioning.

As we begin our journey we are lulled by the silence, hardly noticing the country
rolling past. We read, we nod, we sleep, we awaken.

There is a sound—a cart of kindling crushed on the tracks—
that is what I hear. We stop.

We are stopped for a long time. Passengers begin to worry. Outside men
in uniforms, trainmen and police, patrol the tracks.

We wait. The air conditioning is off. The windows are open. We look
outside, we crane our necks. We see nothing.

Several hours go by. The conductor passes through the cars and tells us:
È morto. A young man has thrown himself on the tracks.

We must change trains. This one must be analyzed for motive, cause—and
effect. Who will cry at the news?

O terra, addio. Was it for love as in history and in myth that a young
man's life vanishes, like a pile of sticks left on the tracks?

Atop a hill

Atop a hill near a stone village
I lie beside you

in a room of pale light
outside our window
one green tree

The cowbell tolls
one two one two
far below are the sea
and ships

but here now
peace.

Additional Acknowledgements

I would like to thank Maureen McLane and Judith Baumel for reading and commenting on my manuscript. I remain in awe of their poetry and am lifted by their encouragement and generosity of spirit.

As always, my thanks to Steve Rubin, my first reader and lifetime inspiration.

Jean P. Moore began her professional career as a high school English teacher. After receiving her Ph.D., she taught for several years at the college level. From there she moved on to a career in management development for a telecommunications firm. Her work led to increasing levels of responsibilities, including her role as executive director of workforce development, a position she held for a number of years. Upon retirement, Jean returned to her first loves: the study of literature and writing.

She has published in several genres, including fiction, non-fiction, and poetry. Most recently, she has concentrated her efforts on novels and poetry, finding the two forms, while very different, complementary. Images of nature, the enduring force of love, and the power of time are recurring themes in both her poetry and fiction. Jean, her husband, Steve, and their black Labrador retriever, Sly, divide their time between Greenwich, Connecticut and Tyringham, Massachusetts where they are frequently found hiking and exploring the Berkshires hills. Jean, a certified yoga instructor, taught for many years in the family's converted barn, aptly named the Yoga Barn.

Website: www.jeanpmoore.com.